80p

1975

B 1976

PROJECT COLLECTION
London Borough of Barnet
School Library Service
9-13 Hendon Lane
N. 3.

About this book

We can learn how the people of earlier times lived by looking at the paintings and drawings which they made about themselves. The pictures in this book will tell you all about the everyday life of a family during Tudor times.

Each member of the household had different activities and duties to perform. The father was the head of the family and ruled the house. The mother had many domestic tasks. She prepared the meals, made all the clothes for her family and looked after the children. If her husband was a nobleman, she would have servants to help her. The daughter of the household learned from her mother how to read, to sew and to play musical instruments. The son might attend a grammar school or he might be educated at home by a tutor. A boy was also expected to learn to ride and to hunt. Look carefully at these pictures. You can find out for yourself how a family lived almost five hundred years ago.

Some of the words printed in *italics* may be new to you. You can look them up in the new word list at the back of the book.

This Sr Robert Hesketh
served kyng Henry the viij in ffraunce
and for his valoure forwardnes acty-
vytie and good service theare was
knighted by thsaid kyng ownn hand
with great comendacons and many
good wordes, w bred great credyt
to hym self, to his ... people, and his
countreye for e...

This Sir Thomas Heskaithe
knight had his sovraigne in Scotland at the
sege of Leeth and theare was sore hurte in
... place and had his ensygne strooken downe
... ... with great comendacons
for his forwardnes and good fate. And was
in his latter dayes anotable great housk...
and benefactor to all men singuler in eny s...
... and greatelie repared the house at ma...
... holme and homes wood and the chappell at
... ...ford

Sr Robert Hesketh knight the onely sonne & heire of Thomas obijt 1539 Feb 8

Dame Grace one of the doughters of John Townley of Townley knighte maried to Sr Robert and by hym had 26 ... yssue 1539

Sr John Holcroft knight maried Anne one of the doughters to ... Standishe of Standyshe esq w whom maried ... ... one of the doughters and heires of Sr James harington knight of ...worthe

Sr Thomas Hes-kaith knight some & gene to Robt, lord of Russed holmes and holmeswood ... kaith houghwick Beron ... Martholme & harwood ... Sheruff of lanc a...
V. F. Eliz: obijt ap...d Russford a° 1587 ...

Dame Alice one of ye doughters to Sr John Holcrofte of Holcroft k knight and had yssue obijt

Robert Hesklaith a seconde sone of Sr Robert maried ... of Preston and had yssue diverse children

Elyne doughter to Sr Robert was maried unto Sr Barton of Barton esq and deceased w out eny yssue of her bodye

... doughter ... maried to ... of Croston ... leastre of Com...

Th... Asheton esq... mar... one of the ... heires to ... of Kenwick ... Salop esq ...ate yss...

AN EYEWITNESS BOOK

The Tudor Family

ANN MITCHELL

WAYLAND PUBLISHERS LONDON

More Eyewitness Books

The Story of the Wheel   Peter Hames
Country Life in the Middle Ages   Penelope Davies
Town Life in the Middle Ages   Penelope Davies
The Printer and his Craft   Helen Wodzicka
The Age of Drake   Leonard W. Cowie
Newgate to Tyburn   Jane Dorner
Growing up in the Middle Ages   Penelope Davies
The Voyages of Captain Cook   Roger Hart
A Victorian Sunday   Jill Hughes
Children of the Industrial Revolution   Penelope Davies

Frontispiece: A Tudor family tree.

SBN 85340 176 4
Copyright © 1972 by
Wayland Publishers Ltd
101 Grays Inn Road London WC1
Printed by C. Tinling & Co. Ltd, Prescot

CONTENTS

1	The Mother	7
2	The Father	27
3	The Son	47
4	The Daughter	61
5	Family Pastimes	71
	Table of Dates	91
	New Words	92
	More Books	94
	Index	95

6

The Mother

In *Tudor* times, families were usually larger than our families. There were many children, and even when they got married they often went on living in their parent's home. Grandparents lived with the family, too. Some boys became apprentices and left home, but most found jobs near their families.

The Tudor mother had a large family to look after. Her biggest job was to manage her household. Without modern vacuum cleaners, washing machines or refrigerators, her life was very busy indeed. A rich noble lady had many servants to help her, but even she needed more skills than most mothers nowadays. Everything the family needed was grown on the farms around the great house. She had to know how to preserve fresh meat and vegetables, how to brew beer, bake bread and make medicines, so that she could instruct her servants properly. Although she did not live in a great house, the farm woman also had all these jobs to do. It was much harder for her because she had no servants, and she had to help her husband on the land as well.

Merchants' wives lived in towns with their husbands and families. Towns in Tudor England were much smaller than they are today, but there were shops and markets where the housewives bought food and household goods.

NOBLEWOMAN'S DRESS. Here is the kind of dress which great Tudor ladies liked to wear. The skirt is very wide, and to make it stand out the lady is wearing a *farthingale*. This was a wide wire hoop fastened around the hips. Around her neck she is wearing a ruff, a fashion which came from Spain. At first, these ruffs were wired to make them stand up. Later, they were stiffened by starch which was invented in the Tudor period.

QUEEN ELIZABETH. Fashions for women were set at court and were copied by most of the rich ladies in the land. As you can see, Queen Elizabeth I is wearing a wired lace collar which reaches almost to the top of her head. Dresses and hair styles were very fancy. As the Queen grew older, she began to wear a wig, so wigs became fashionable. Children with long hair were sometimes attacked by thieves who cut it off and sold it to wig makers!

CARING FOR CHILDREN. The Tudor lady had more to do than worry about her appearance. In this picture you can see twin sisters, the Cholmondeley sisters, nursing their babies. Children of wealthy Tudor families were looked after by a nursemaid most of the time, but their mother might play with them, teach them to read, or sing to them. They liked some of the nursery rhymes that we still sing—"Sing a Song of Sixpence," "Three Blind Mice" and "Ding Dong Bell, Pussy's in the Well."

GREAT HOUSES. Besides her children, a Tudor noblewoman had her home to look after. She might live in a great house like this one. It was her job to run the house and manage the large number of servants, cooks and gardeners. She always had to be ready to receive crowds of guests. Great lords and ladies liked to travel and to visit one another in their stately homes. She might even receive a visit from Queen Elizabeth, who spent months travelling around England on her royal *progresses*.

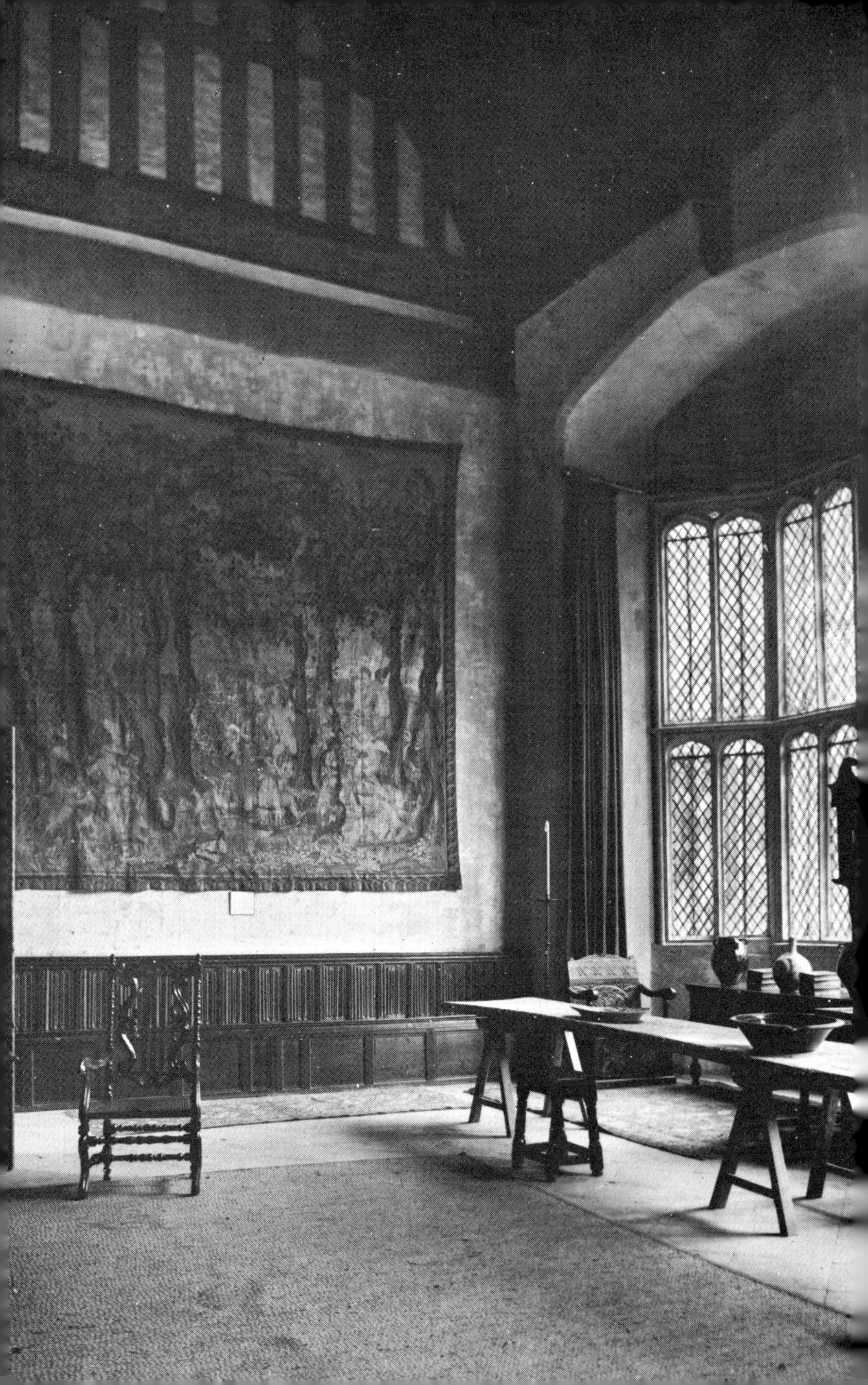

GREAT HALLS. On the left you can see the great hall of a grand Tudor house, Compton Wynates. It belonged to Sir William Compton who was a good friend of Henry VIII (1509–47). Here large banquets were held; many people could sit down to dinner together at the long table. The lady of such a house would serve enormous feasts with eight or nine courses which often lasted long into the night. Notice the tapestry on the wall. Tapestries were used for decoration and helped to keep large rooms warm.

FOUR-POSTER BEDS. When guests stayed at a nobleman's house, they often shared one large bed, like the four-poster in this picture below. This bed is so big that it became famous; a dozen people could sleep in it at once. It is called the Great Bed of Ware, and you can see it in the Victoria and Albert Museum in London. These beds were made of beautifully carved wood. Thick curtains were hung from the roof or "tester" to keep out draughts. Would you like to sleep in such a bed? You can imagine how difficult it was to heat these huge homes with nothing but log fires.

NEEDLEWORK. Noblewomen spent much of their leisure time sewing. In Tudor times English embroidery was famous all over Europe. Housewives were proud of their careful work on cushions, coverlets and clothing. You can see one woman spinning, another stitching, and a third doing embroidery on a frame. Notice the baby at the back of the room; he is learning to walk in a special frame on wheels.

14

MEAL TIMES. One of the mother's most important jobs in a great house was to run the kitchen and plan the meals for the family and servants. She also had to organize lavish banquets for her many guests. In this picture you can see a banquet in progress in the great hall. Behind the scenes the servants are busy in the kitchen. The cook's assistant is roasting the meat on a spit over an open fire. Three serving boys are taking silver dishes of food into the great hall. Rich people had fine tableware; they ate off silver plate and drank from Venetian glass. But they only had knives and spoons—no one had yet invented forks.

16

KNOT GARDEN. The picture on the left shows a "knot garden". Shrubs and herbs of many sizes, shapes and smells are grouped together to form a pretty design rather like a knot. Notice the well on the left: here the gardener could draw water for the shrubs. All kinds of herbs were grown in the garden. The lady of the house knew a great deal about them. She knew how to use them in cooking, how to make medicines from them in case her family were ill, and how to use them in make-up. Ladies liked to wear make-up and powder on their faces to copy the pale complexion of Queen Elizabeth.

FLOWERS. A Tudor writer tells us, "In summer gentlewomen will carry in their hands nosegays and posies or flowers to smell at." A nobleman's wife had to supervise the large garden and give orders to the gardeners. In these lower pictures the ladies are gathering flowers to take indoors. Ladies also used flowers to make perfume; they put flowers in their gloves to make their hands smell sweet.

Een burghers wijf   Een burghers rijck wijf   Een ionghe dochter   Een

TOWN AND COUNTRY WOMEN. The merchants' wives in the picture on the left are well dressed but notice that their clothes are much simpler than those of the noblewomen. Instead of wide ruffs and farthingale skirts, they have simple dresses with high stiff collars. The woman on the right is a country woman and she is wearing a scarf or *muffler* over her mouth. Most of England's roads were mud tracks, and travellers could easily get a mouthful of dust when the weather was dry.

MERCHANTS' HOMES. Merchants' wives, too, had households and servants to look after. The homes of rich merchants were quite large, though not nearly as big as mansions like Compton Wynates. Many merchants had houses in the Strand in London, overlooking the River Thames. This map of the Strand was drawn in the time of Queen Elizabeth. Notice the open fields: London then was tiny compared with London today.

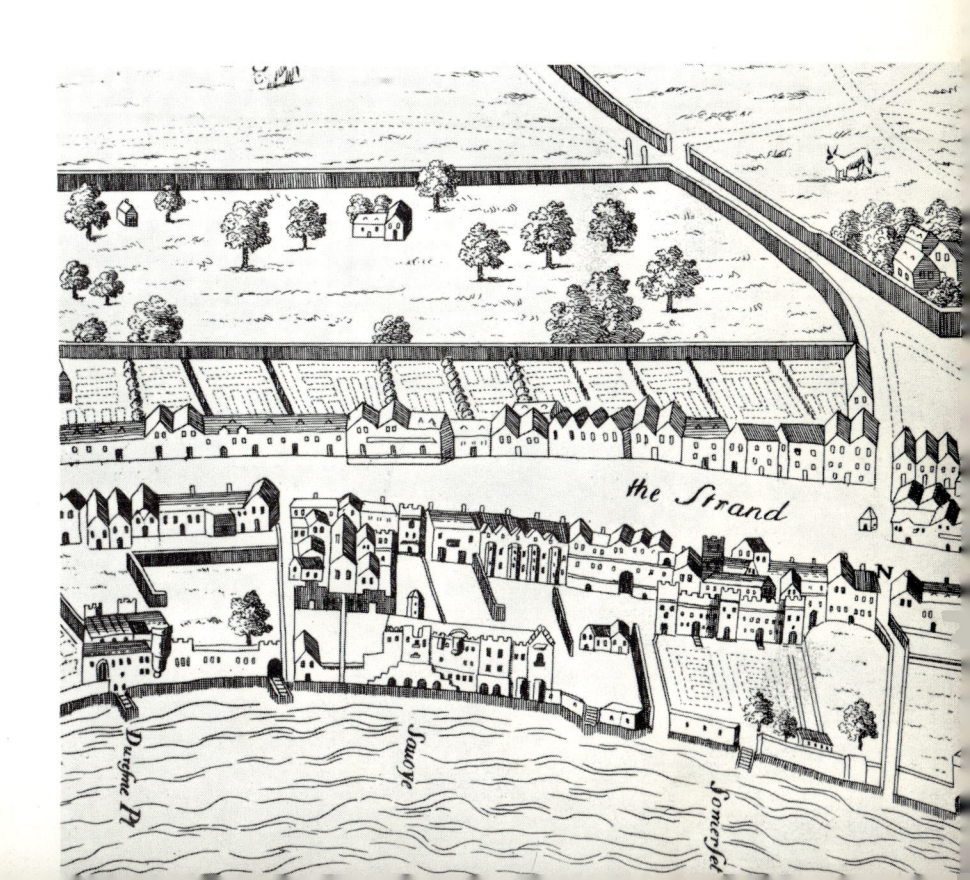

BILLINGESGATE

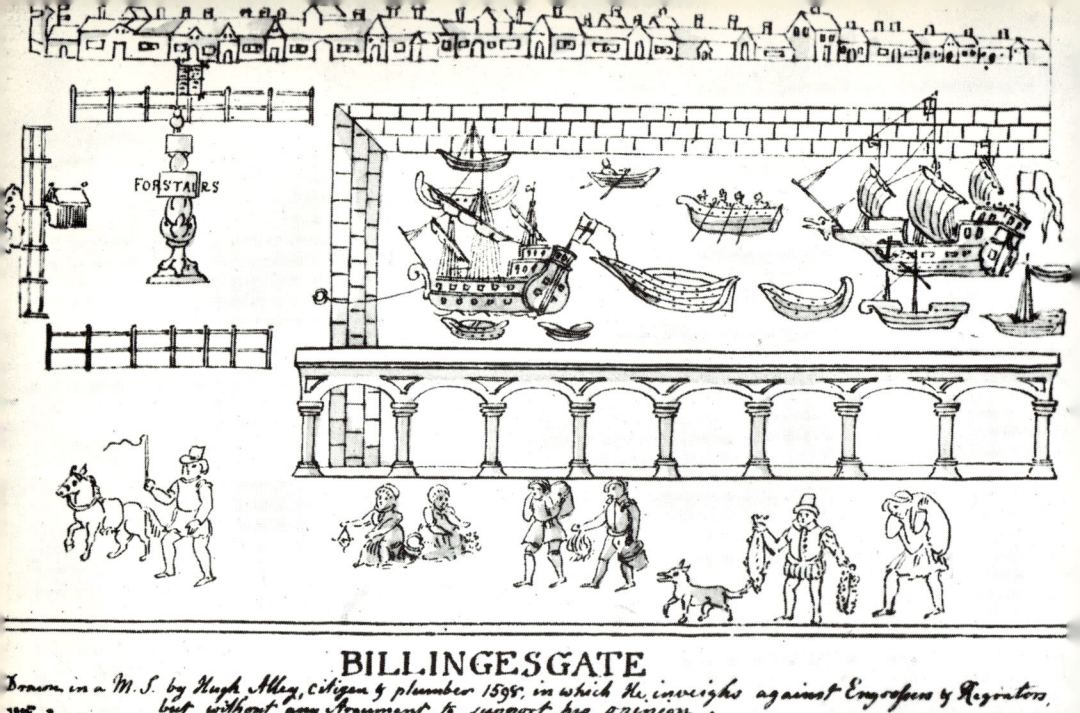

Drawn in a M.S. by Hugh Alley, citizen & plumber 1598, in which he inveighs against Engrossers & Regrators, but without any argument to support his opinion.

MARKETS. Merchants lived in towns like London, York, Bristol, or Coventry. Their wives did not have gardens for growing food, so they sent their servants to buy food from markets. The upper picture shows Billingsgate in London, where fish was sold. It is by the River Thames, so fish could be taken off the boats. Below is Eastcheap, London's meat market. Notice the farmer bringing his cattle and sheep to market. On the left, a merchant's wife and her servant have come to do their shopping.

A FARMHOUSE KITCHEN. Life for the wives of farmers and peasants was very different. A farmer's wife did not have a great house to run, just a small timber cottage. She had no servants; she did everything herself, without any modern machines to help her. Here she is in her kitchen. There is no running hot water, so she is boiling up water in the bucket hanging over the fire. Notice the firewood in the corner of the room. She needs the bellows to make the fire hotter so she can cook the fish in the basin.

Rustica Anglicana   *Modus vendendi Lupos pisces apud Anglos*   *Paremptitius*

COUNTRY MARKETS. Farmers' wives did their shopping at country markets. In the picture opposite, you can see the fish seller cleaning the fish. The man with the bucket is about to draw water from the well. There would be no running water in his small cottage. The picture below the market shows a farmer's wife riding home with a basket full of provisions. She is wearing a muffler, too.

HAYMAKING. The farmer's wife had to help her husband on the farm. Harvest was the busiest time of the year for the farmer. In the picture below, she is helping her husband with the haymaking. She would also have to milk the cows, fetch the eggs, and cook meals for the farmer and his men. Preparing meals was not an easy task for the farmers wife. She had to bake her own bread, brew her own beer, and make butter and cheese by churning milk.

SPINNING AND WEAVING. Spinning and weaving wool was done by most country women in Tudor England. In the top picture the woman is spinning the sheeps' wool into thread. Below, you can see the spun wool hanging in bales on the wall and wound into balls in the basket. The woman is weaving the thread into cloth on the loom. When it is finished, the length of cloth will be sent to the merchant in the town. The wool trade was England's biggest industry.

WASHDAY. Here are country women doing their washing in the village stream. The woman standing in the water is scrubbing her washing on a stone to get it really clean. They had to beat their washing to get the water out. Another woman is laying out the sheets on the ground to bleach them in the sun. There were no such things as washing machines, soap powder, irons or mangles.

26

The Father

The father was the head of the family and he ruled his household with complete authority. He expected his family to behave during the week, to go to church on Sunday, and to obey him at all times. He was also very strict with the servants, and disobedient servants could be fined, dismissed or beaten. Naughty children were often beaten as well.

All fathers worked to support their families. The nobleman had large farms where his labourers raised sheep and cattle and grew crops. He rented out some of his land to small farmers. He also made money by selling flour, wool, meat and milk to townspeople.

The small farmer or country labourer earned a living by working on the land. His wife and children often helped him with his many tasks. As well as keeping a cow, a pig and a few hens, and growing crops, he might spin wool and weave it into cloth. Merchants bought wool from the countryfolk and sold it in the towns, especially in London. Sometimes they sent the cloth to Europe when they could get a good price for it. In exchange they bought silks and spices, glass and jewellery to sell in England. Merchants often grew very rich.

Poor farmers spent most of their time with their families. But merchants, like modern businessmen, had to leave home to travel on business. A nobleman also had to leave his family to visit his estates, attend at court, or help govern the kingdom.

NOBLEMEN. Here is the father of a noble family. Tudor noblemen liked fine colourful clothes, and they often outshone the ladies. Suits were made of heavy silk and velvet and embroidered with jewels. The most fashionable men wore scent and earrings. This man is very proud of his gaily decorated breeches and spurs. Men in Tudor times liked to wear tall hats with brightly coloured feathers, "perking up like the spear, or shaft of a steeple."

COURTIERS. Most great men in Tudor times held positions at court. They had to spend much time away from home to attend the king or queen. In the top picture you can see *courtiers* escorting Queen Elizabeth through London. Many noblemen took part in affairs of state and helped to govern the country. Below you can see them holding a conference in Somerset House.

JOUSTING. There were not many wars in Tudor times, but noblemen were trained in battle in case they had to take up a military command. To practise their fighting and prove their bravery, they took part in dangerous tournaments in front of the court. Both these riders and horses are protected by heavy armour. The jousters use their lances to knock each other off their horses.

MERCHANTS. The wealthy merchant in the picture on the left is wearing richly embroidered clothes, although they are simpler than the nobleman's clothes. Merchants in Tudor England were very prosperous and they traded with other countries in many parts of the world. They lived in large town houses built of brick or stone. Their businesses and shops were on the ground floor. The Lord Mayor of London was chosen from the leading merchants of the City. He is in the upper picture on the left.

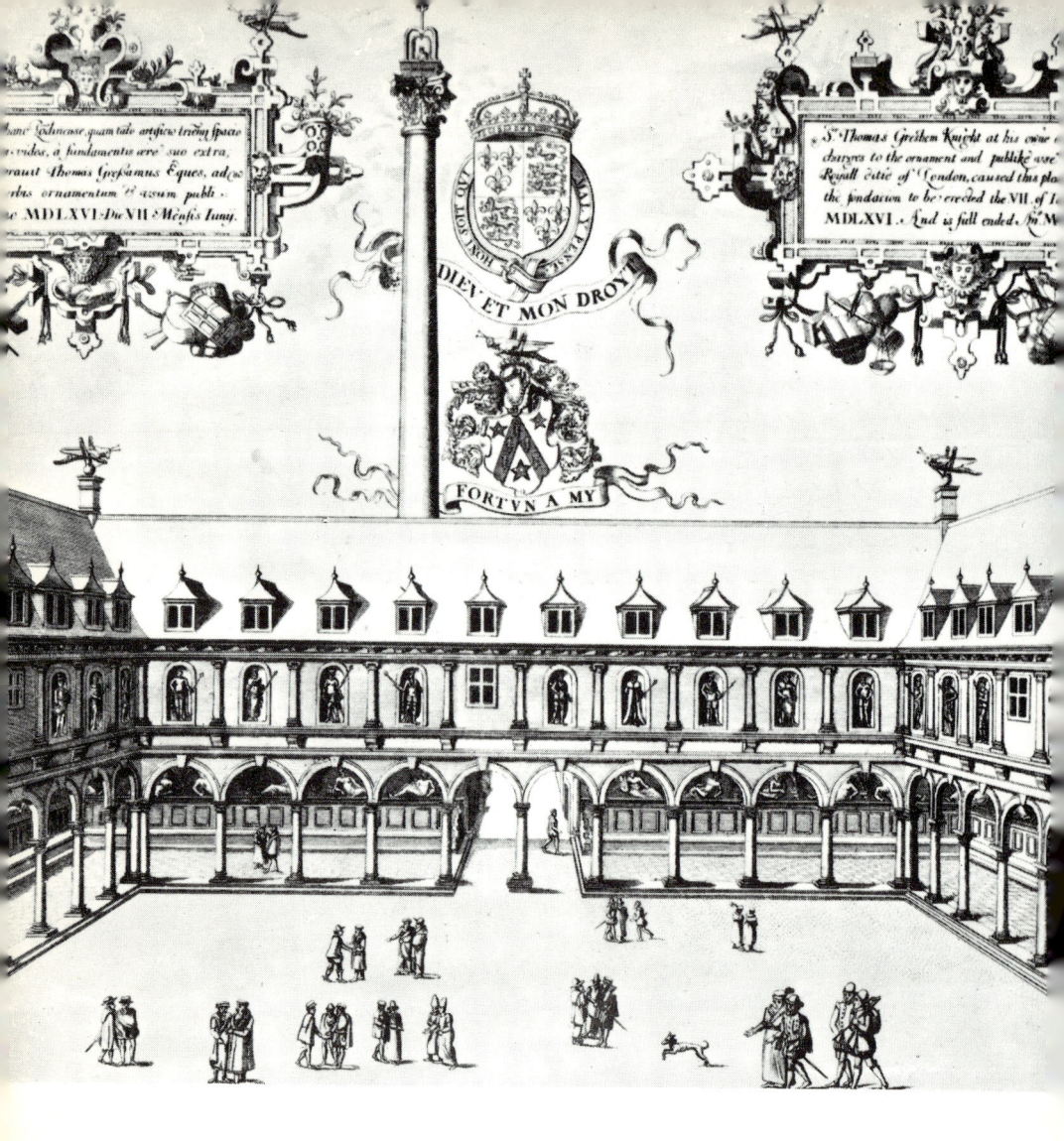

ROYAL EXCHANGE. This is the Royal Exchange in London, where merchants could buy and sell goods. A bell rang at midday and six o'clock in the evening, calling merchants to hear the news of the day and do business in its hundred shops. On the ground level behind the pillars, shoppers could buy everything they needed. The Exchange was not only open to merchants but to anyone who wanted to stroll or gossip. There was music in the courtyard on Sunday evenings. Football was forbidden in the courtyard because it was so rough and played without rules.

32

COACH TRAVEL. Rich merchants travelled a great deal around the countryside to sell their goods. Going by coach was a fast way of travelling in Tudor times, but it was not very comfortable. The carriages had no springs and the dirt roads were full of rocks, so it was a very bumpy ride. You can see the bad road in this picture. And there was always the danger of being robbed by highwaymen.

INNS. A merchant on a long journey would have to spend the night at an inn. Although the roads were bad, the inns were often excellent. Here a merchant could expect a warm welcome from the innkeeper and his family. The merchant in the top picture is enjoying the company of some village people. They are drinking tankards of ale and smoking clay pipes. After Sir Walter Raleigh (1552–1618) brought tobacco from America, smoking became a popular habit in Tudor England.

SHOPS. On the opposite page are two shops, a tailor's and a shoemaker's. The shoemaker has just finished making a pair of boots. On the wall above them are pieces of wood which he will put inside the boots to make them keep their shape. The tailor is cutting cloth to make another cloak like the ones you can see hanging up on the wall. The shopkeepers and their families lived above the shops.

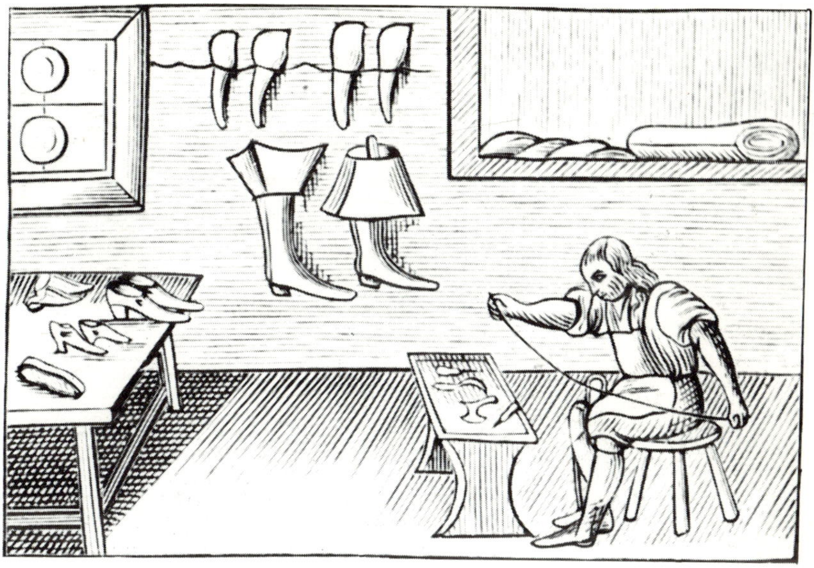

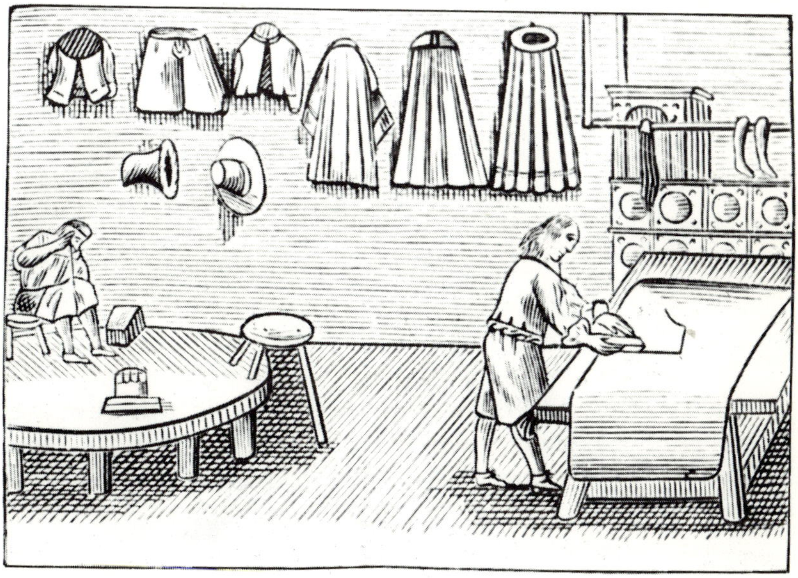

STREET SELLERS. This man sells hats but he does not have a shop. His family lives in a very small house and he spends his day walking up and down the streets shouting out his wares. He also sells all kind of baskets and fans. He is carrying so much that he has to wear several hats on his head at once!

MACHINAMENTVM VT NON VVLGARE, SICVT OPINAMVR
ITA SINGVLARE IN EIACVLANDA AQVA, ADVERSVS
INCENDIA: MAXIME CVM FLAMMA SVPERANTE, NVLLI
PROPIVS AD AEDES PATET ADITVS-

FIREMEN. These firemen have a dangerous job. They are putting out the flames in a house with one of the first fire engines. There were many fires in Tudor towns. The houses were made of wood and built so close together that they easily caught alight. In London, water was pumped by a machine under London Bridge to points called "conduits". Women fetched water from the conduits and brought it to the firemen. You can see the women in this picture running with their buckets to the conduit so they can fill up the barrel of water.

BELLMAN. After dark, the streets of Tudor towns were dangerous places. Most of the streets were unlit, and thieves and *footpads* hid in the dark alleys ready to rob the passersby. Bellmen or watchmen patrolled the streets at night. This bellman has brought his dog with him. There were few chiming clocks, so the bellman also called out the time to the citizens every hour.

FARMERS. Nine out of ten families in Tudor England lived in the country and farmed the land. Each village was usually surrounded by three large fields, and these were divided into strips where different crops were grown. The rich squire in the opposite picture owns a great deal of land. He does not farm it himself, but pays labourers to work for him. He is using a surveyor's instrument to measure his land.

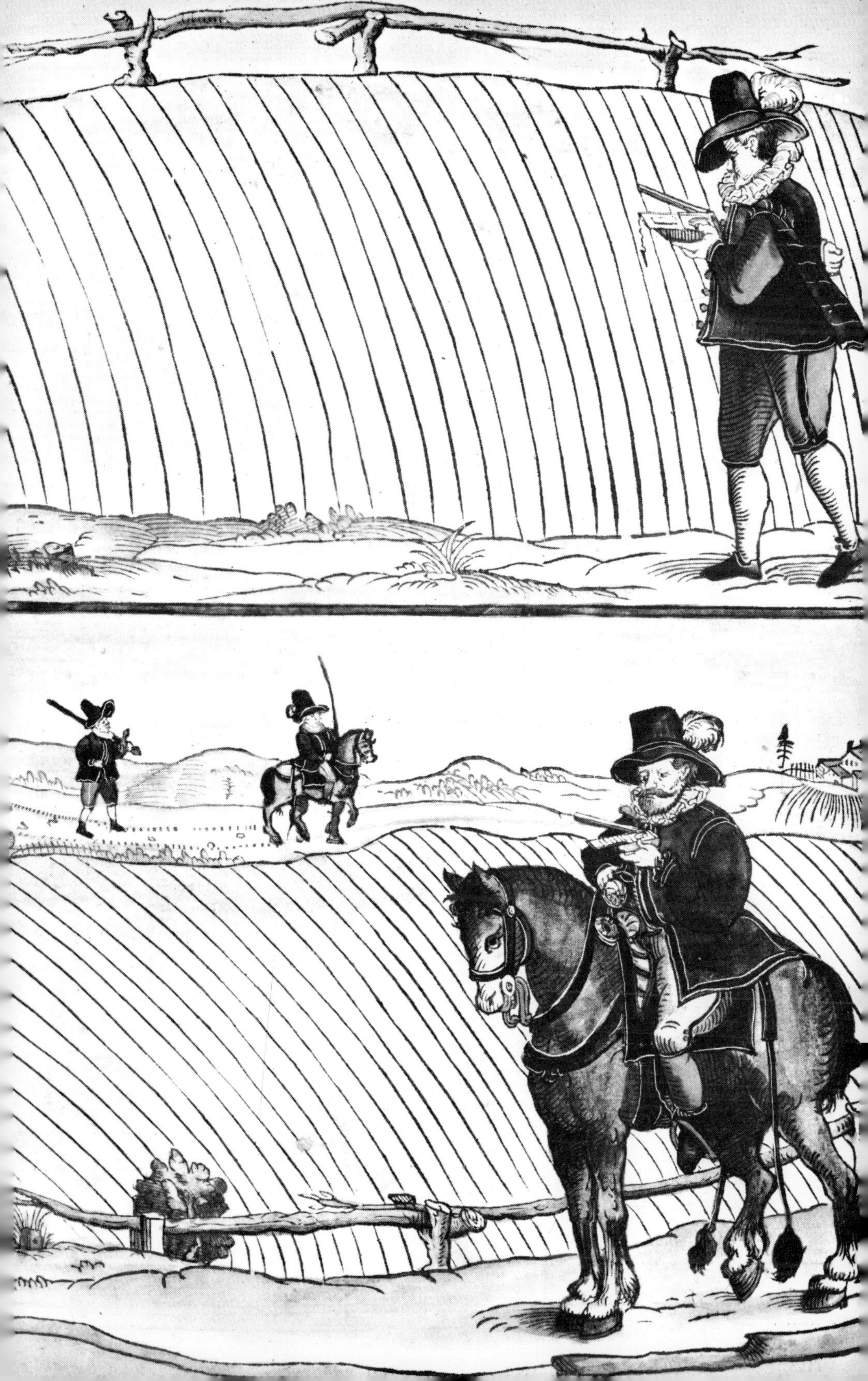

FARM LABOURERS. Farm labourers had to work very hard. In those days they had no modern machinery such as tractors. Here the labourers are harvesting the corn. The farmer is giving orders while the men cut the corn with sickles. Their wives are helping them to tie it into bundles. Next, the corn will be threshed to separate the grain from the chaff. The grain will be taken to the miller, who will grind it into flour.

DYEING. Many poor farmers made woollen cloth to earn extra money. Women and children spun the wool, but dyeing the cloth was usually the father's job. This man is dipping his cloth into a large vat of coloured dye. He uses the long stick to stir the dye. The man in the background is hanging up the newly dyed cloth on long poles to dry.

BLACKSMITHS. Blacksmiths were kept very busy in Tudor villages, shoeing horses and making metal farm tools. Most people travelled about on horseback, and on the farms horses did all the work a tractor does today. Here, the blacksmiths are hammering a piece of iron on an anvil. On the left is a forge where they can heat the metal to make it soft. It was easier to hammer softened metal into shape.

VETERINARY SURGEONS. In the countryside the vet was a very important person, as he is today. Often he was the local blacksmith. Tudor families liked to keep animals as pets, but on the farm, horses, oxen and sheep dogs had to work. If they were ill, the farmer called in the vet to cure them. In this picture the vet is using a funnel to pour medicine down the dog's throat. He carries extra medicines in flasks which are hanging from his belt. Many of the cures were no good.

SOLDIERS. Although there were few battles in Tudor England, some men had to leave their families to join the army. Each part of England had its own militia. Soldiers did not see their families very often, but they might be sent home in the winter when the campaigning season was over. They were badly paid and had little to eat. Here you can see them having their meal in an army camp. Notice the musket on the ground. Guns like this had only just been invented. Villagers still had to practise archery.

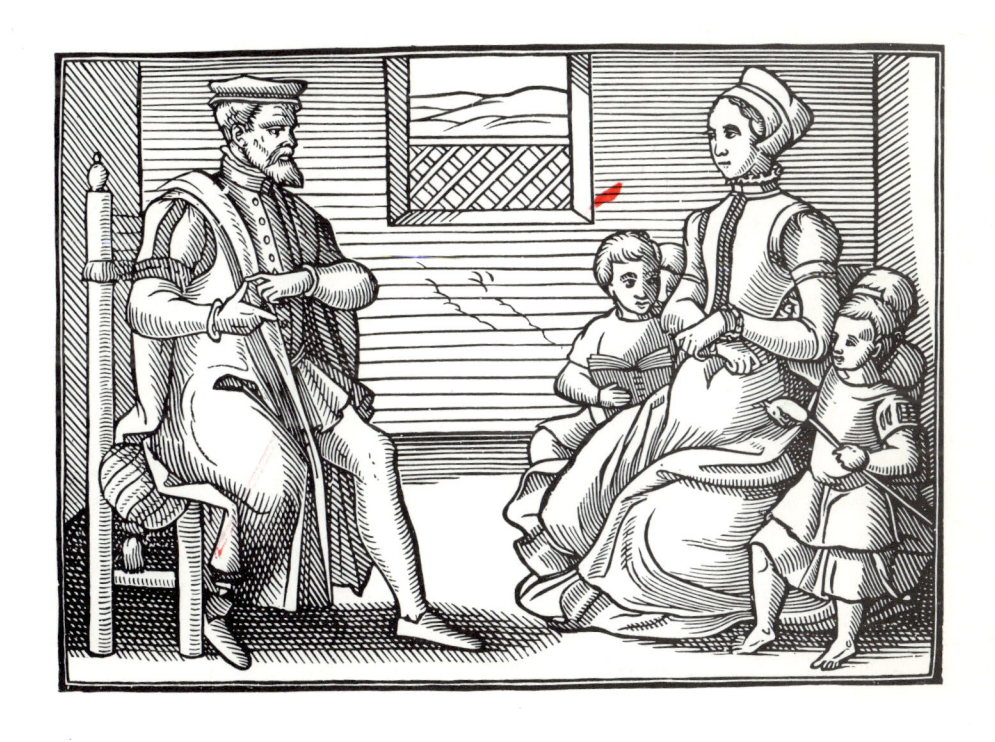

FATHERS AT HOME. We have looked at all kinds of Tudor men—statesmen, merchants, craftsmen, farmers, and soldiers. All Tudor fathers had important duties in the home. They ruled over the household very strictly. Here is a *puritan* father. He is teaching his family the beliefs of his religion. His son is holding the Bible. Henry VIII had allowed the Bible to be written in English instead of just Latin as before.

46

The Son

Boys from rich families lived very differently from boys of poor families. Noblemen's sons were brought up to be gentlemen. As young boys, they were taught reading and writing by their parents or by private tutors. When they were seven years old they were sent to school, together with the sons of rich merchants. But boys from poor families usually never went to school at all. They started work at a very early age and were thought to have no need of education.

From early childhood, boys were expected to behave like adults. They wore exactly the same clothes as their fathers—feather hats, *doublets* and breeches. The eldest son was even trained to do the same job as his father. He usually inherited all his father's property and became the head of the family when his father died.

Boys had to learn the skills they would use when they were grown up. The rich boy learned to hunt and joust. Some boys were apprenticed to master-craftsmen to learn a trade. If they had more education, they might become clerks, doctors, lawyers, or merchants. The poorest boys were sent to farms and to learn the work of a farm labourer. The youngest sons often had a hard time learning a trade or business. Their families might not have enough money left to pay for their education. Many of them left home to join the army, either in England or on the Continent, or to go to sea.

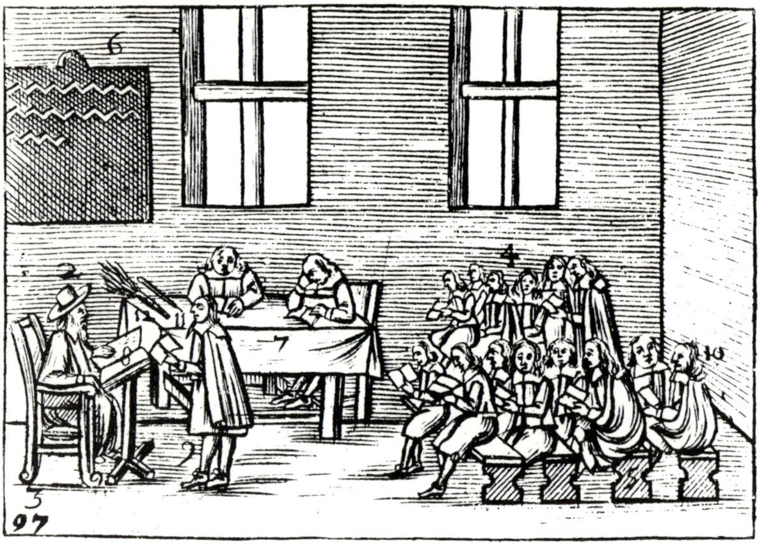
6
2
7
4
5
97

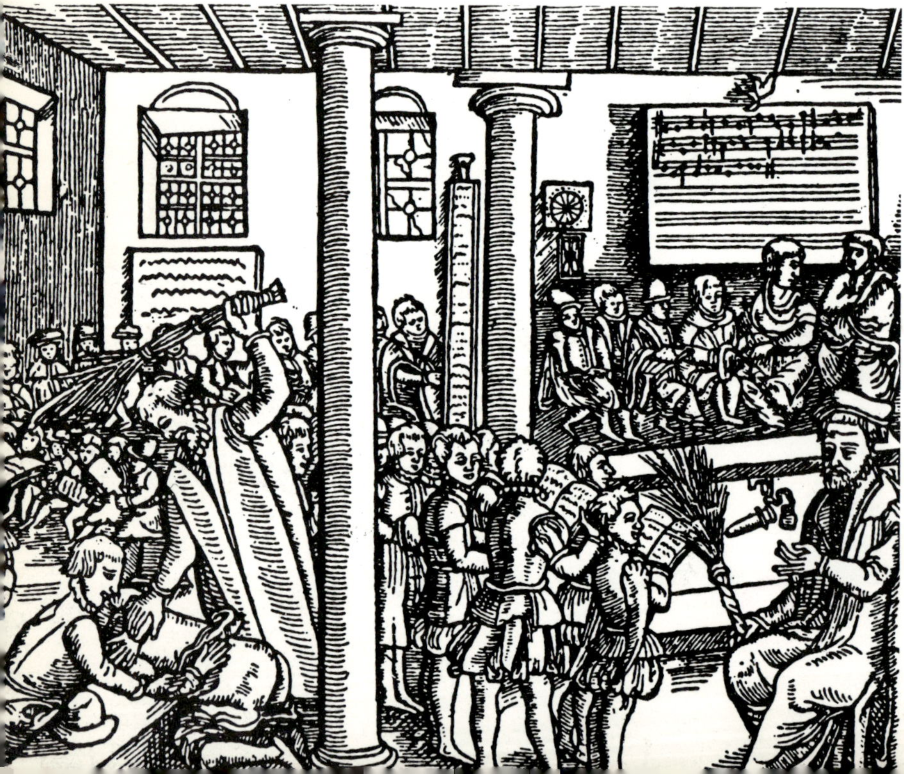

SCHOOLS. The pictures on the opposite page show boys' schools in Elizabethan times. All the boys were taught together in one room. They spent more time learning Latin than anything else. In the lower picture, a boy on the left is reading aloud to one section of the class. Boys also learned music and singing at school. You can see some music on the wall in the back of the room. A master is beating one pupil. Discipline was strict, and boys were beaten if they did not learn their lessons, or if they misbehaved. Parents had to provide their sons with quill pens made of feathers, and special knives to trim them with. In winter boys had to bring their own candles.

GAMES AT SCHOOL. The school day was long and there were few holidays. Boys started classes at six in the morning and finished at half past five in the afternoon, including Saturdays. They had a fortnight's holiday at Christmas and at Easter. There was not much time to play, so Tudor boys made the most of their games. Here you can see them playing with rattles and a hobby-horse. On the right is a more unusual game—a boy blows bubbles while his friends try to catch them on a cushion.

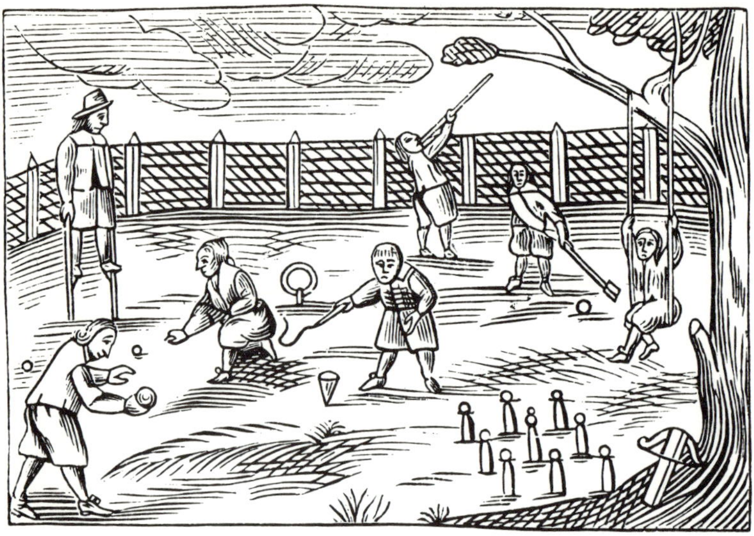

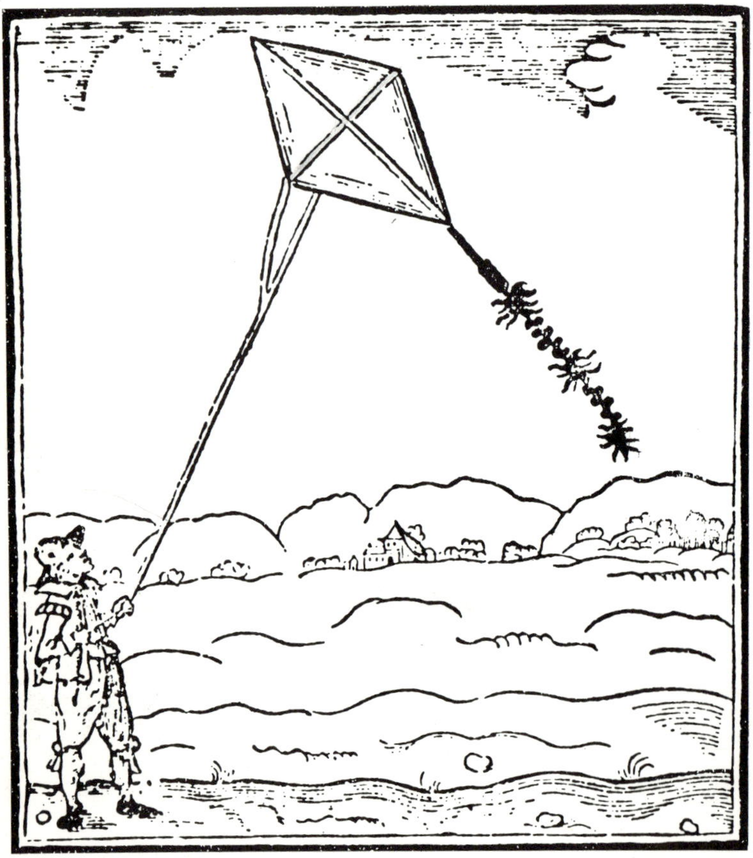

BOYS' GAMES. The boys in the pictures opposite are playing all kinds of games. Above, one boy is blowing peas through a pea shooter. Another is playing skittles, one has a spinning top, and a third is walking on stilts. These games do not look very different from those of today. The boy below is seeing how high he can fly his kite. How many games can you count altogether?

WINTER SPORTS. Boys had plenty of fun in winter when the rivers were frozen. In London, they liked to skate on the Thames and toboggan on the surrounding frozen marshes. Here the streets are covered with snow, and this boy is riding with his father on a sledge shaped like a swan. Their servant runs alongside. The father must be a rich merchant to afford such a fine sledge and horse.

FISHING. When they were not at school, most Tudor boys liked to fish in the rivers and ponds near their towns and villages. Even in London fishermen caught salmon and many other kinds of fish in the Thames. One boy has just hooked a fish which he is going to put in the basket. He will take it home for his mother to cook, or preserve in salt. Most Tudor families ate lots of fish, since fresh meat was very expensive.

APPRENTICES. When they finished school, a few rich boys went to university at Oxford or Cambridge, but most boys had to learn a trade. They were apprenticed to master-craftsmen for seven years. The masters were almost like fathers to their apprentices. They made sure that the boys worked hard, learned the craft, went to church on Sunday and behaved themselves in public. Here you can see two tailor's apprentices learning to stitch clothes. Other craftsmen included masons, carpenters, shoemakers, jewellers, glass-makers, printers, paper-makers, and armourers.

The English Gentleman

SPES IN CAELIS

PES IN TERRIS

Generoso Germine Germino

ENGLISH GENTLEMEN. In a noble family a boy was sent to school not only to learn to read and write, but also to become a gentleman. There was more to being a gentleman than wearing fine clothes and carrying a smart walking stick. The book on the opposite page shows the behaviour expected of him. He had to be good tempered, well-mannered, well-educated and he had to know how to ride and hunt. Gentlemen also became army officers and went on dangerous sea voyages.

PAGE BOYS. Sons from noble families were often sent to be trained as page boys in the great houses of other lords. They would be taught the correct behaviour and manners which they would need to know when they were grown up. Then they would take up positions at court in the sevice of the king or queen. In this picture you can see a gentleman asking the page to fetch more wine for his lady.

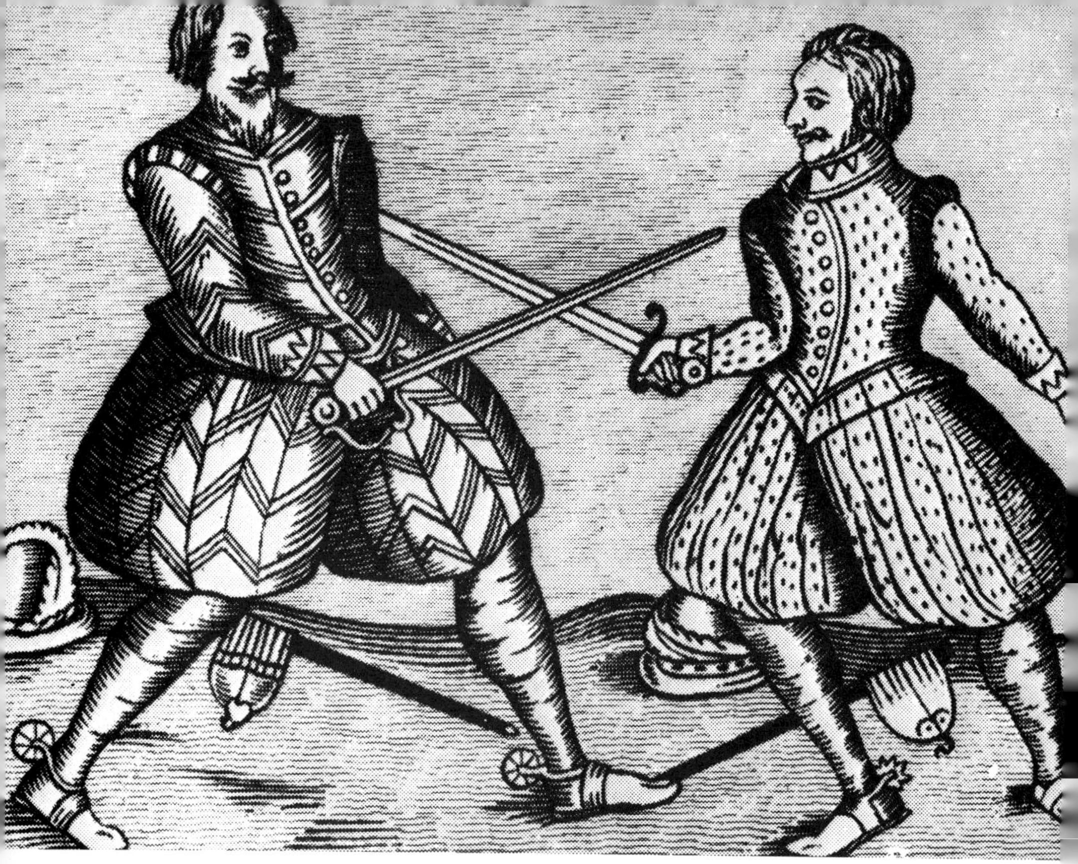

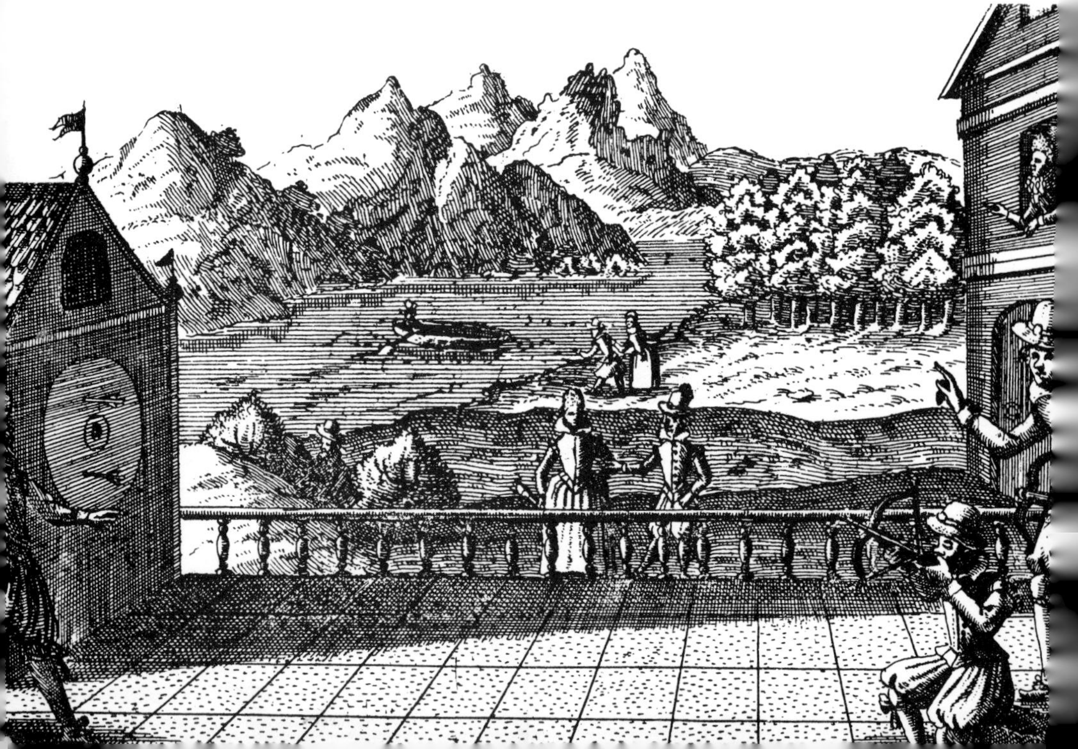

The whetstone

FENCING AND ARCHERY. Fencing was another art the Tudor gentleman was expected to know, because duels were very common. You can see duellists in the top picture on the opposite page. The page boy above is carrying a whetstone. He will scrape the fencers' swordblades on this stone to sharpen them. Tudor boys also had to master archery. The noblemen's sons opposite are practising their archery on the terrace of a great house. They are trying very hard to hit the bulls-eye in the middle of the target.

KITCHEN BOYS. In the countryside boys from poor families often found work in the great country houses. They could train to be serving men, gardeners, stewards or chefs. Boys in the kitchen worked very hard. They washed the dishes, swept the floors and helped the cooks with their many different jobs. Here, two boys are roasting fish and meat on a spit. Notice the ducks, geese, and sausages hanging up, ready for cooking.

SHEPHERDS. Beyond the fields surrounding the village were common lands where sheep and cattle could graze. Some poor boys in the village worked as shepherds. These shepherds are both carrying crooks and wearing slings around their necks. They use their slings to carry injured lambs who cannot walk. The sheep wore bells so that shepherds could hear them. Shepherds' dogs were trained to answer the music of their masters' reed pipes and the sound of the bells.

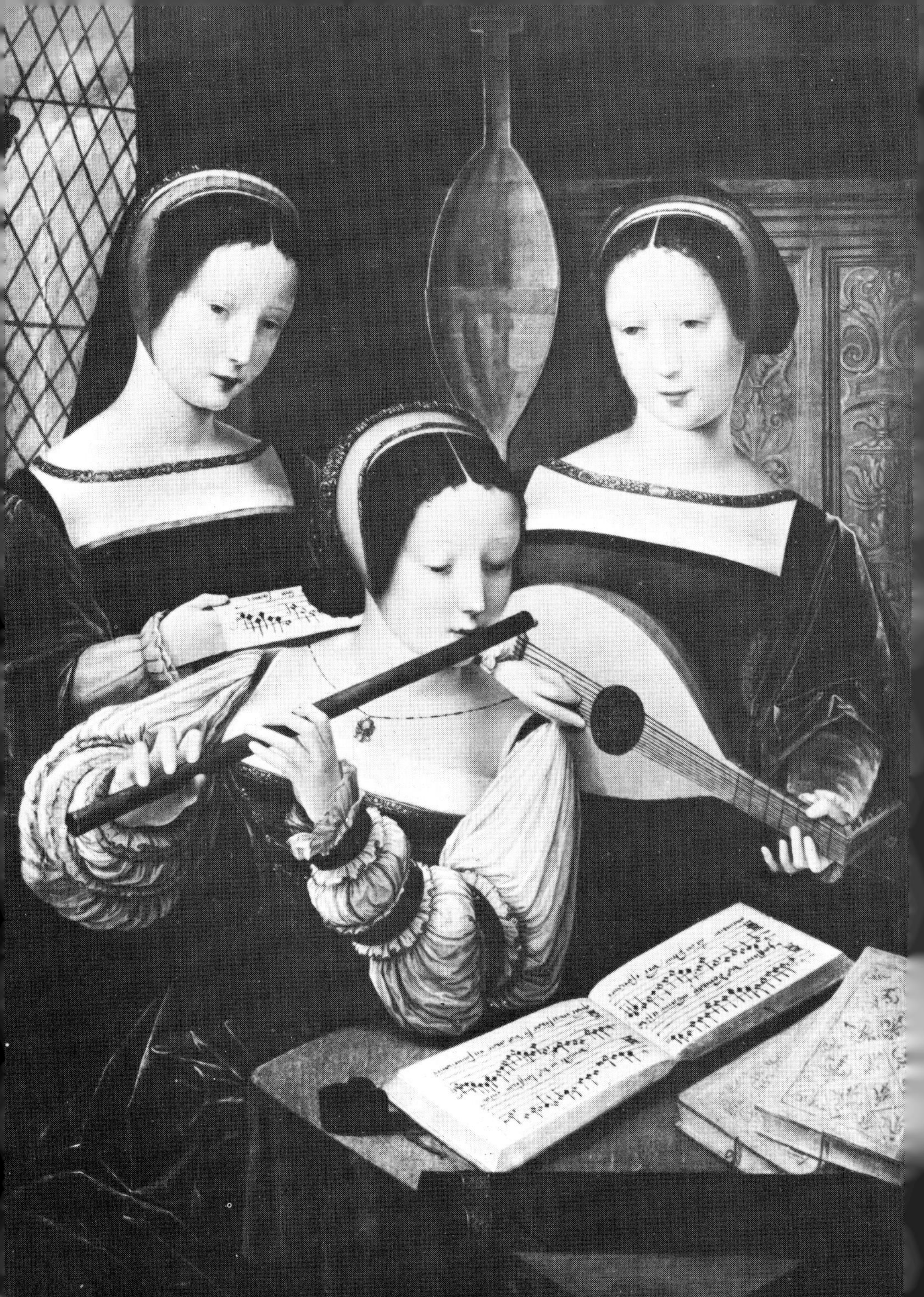

The Daughter

Girls did not have as much freedom as their brothers. They were not nearly as free as girls are today. There were no jobs in offices, factories, hospitals or schools as there are today. All girls were expected to marry and have families. Until they married they lived at home where their mothers taught them everything they would have to know when they became mothers themselves.

Girls were not as well-educated as boys, but some of them from wealthy families did go to school. They could attend a *petty school* where small children were taught to read and write. A few even went to boarding school. But most girls from wealthy families took lessons from a tutor with their brothers. Many Tudor girls, even the daughters of country farmers, could read and write. If they did not have tutors or go to school, their mothers taught them to read. There were few printed books in Tudor England, so children used horn books; these were pieces of wood, covered with a layer of animal horn. The letters of the alphabet and the Lord's Prayer were printed on them. Not many girls were as clever as Queen Elizabeth who was already learning French, Italian and Latin when she was nine. Daughters of peasant farmers and craftsmen rarely had the chance to learn to read and write. Instead, they were taught their parents' work—spinning, shopkeeping, or farming.

ENGLISH GENTLEWOMEN. In noble families, daughters were brought up to be ladies. They did not have women's magazines, but this book shows what a young lady was expected to become: graceful, well-behaved, well-dressed and religious. There were no special clothes for girls, and the young lady in this picture is wearing the same kind of embroidered dress and stiff, white ruff as her mother would wear. She is carrying a little prayer book.

MUSIC. Music was an important part of a Tudor girl's education. She was expected to sing and to play a musical instrument. Girls of wealthy families would be taught to sing and play by a tutor at home. In the lower picture one girl is singing and her sisters are accompanying her on the flute and *virginals*. The young ladies above are making music at a spring festival. They have formed a small orchestra. One girl is playing the harp, and another has a *viol*. Two girls on the left are playing a *lute* and a flute.

DANCING. A country girl would learn simple jigs and country dances at the village festivals. Above, farmers' daughters are dancing at a May Day celebration. The lady and gentleman in the cart are dressed as the King and Queen of the May. For the daughter of a wealthy family, learning to dance was more difficult. She would have a dancing master to teach her all the complicated steps she needed to know to perform the stately court dances.

WEAVING. A girl brought up on a farm learned all the jobs that her mother did. She would have to know how to do these tasks when she became a housewife. Many country farmers and their wives earned a living by spinning and weaving, and they taught their daughters this trade. In the opposite picture above, a girl is spinning wool into yarn. Below she takes the yarn to her father, who is working the loom for weaving cloth.

65

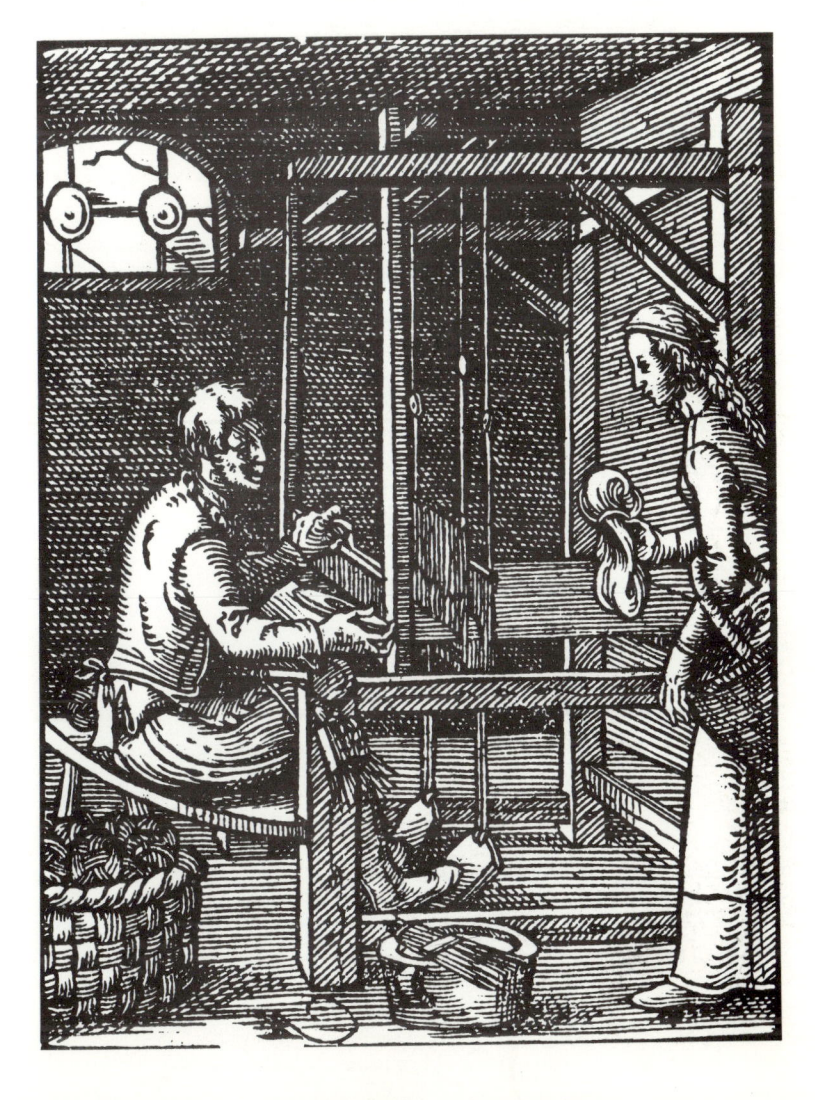

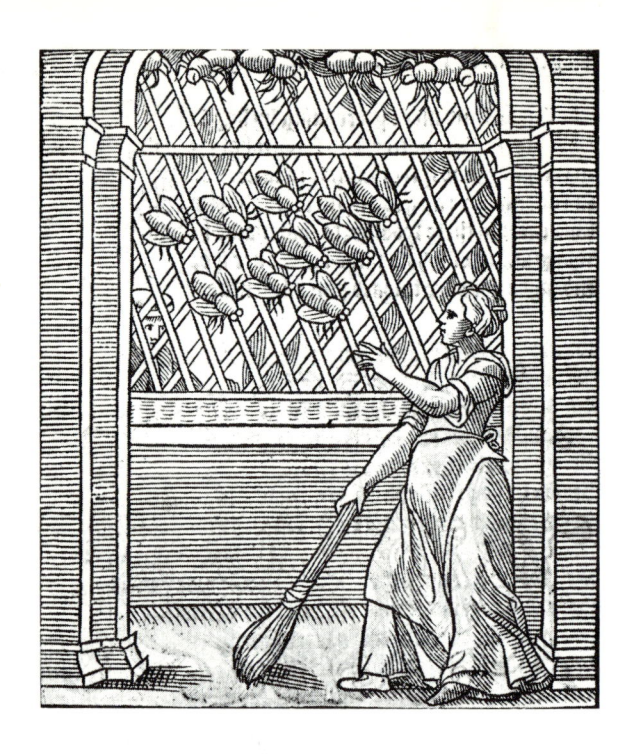

HOUSEMAIDS. In the great houses, daughters of servants became housemaids as soon as they were old enough to carry out their tasks. They had to get up very early in the morning as they had many rooms to dust and floors to scrub. The girl above is having trouble brushing away the flies! Below a chambermaid is making the big four-poster bed. She uses a stick to smooth out the sheets.

COURTING. Whether she was rich or poor, every girl expected to get married and become a housewife and mother. She would have to stay with her parents until she married as there was no job she could do outside the home. Here the daughter of a rich man is being courted by a wealthy merchant. He looks much older than she is. He had to earn enough money to be able to support her before he could hope to marry her.

DOWRY CHESTS. Even if a girl married a rich man, her parents would have to give money and goods to her husband. They might give sheets, blankets and furnishings for the home. They were called a *dowry* and were kept in a dowry chest like the one above. Every nobleman expected to receive a good dowry with his bride. If the parents could not afford a dowry, their daughter might have to marry a poor man.

WEDDINGS. Look at the top of the next page: a girl from a poor family is marrying a cobbler. The wedding is very simple and there are not many friends present. But the rich young lady below has a beautiful wedding dress and two bridesmaids. Her other friends watch anxiously as she walks to the altar in the church.

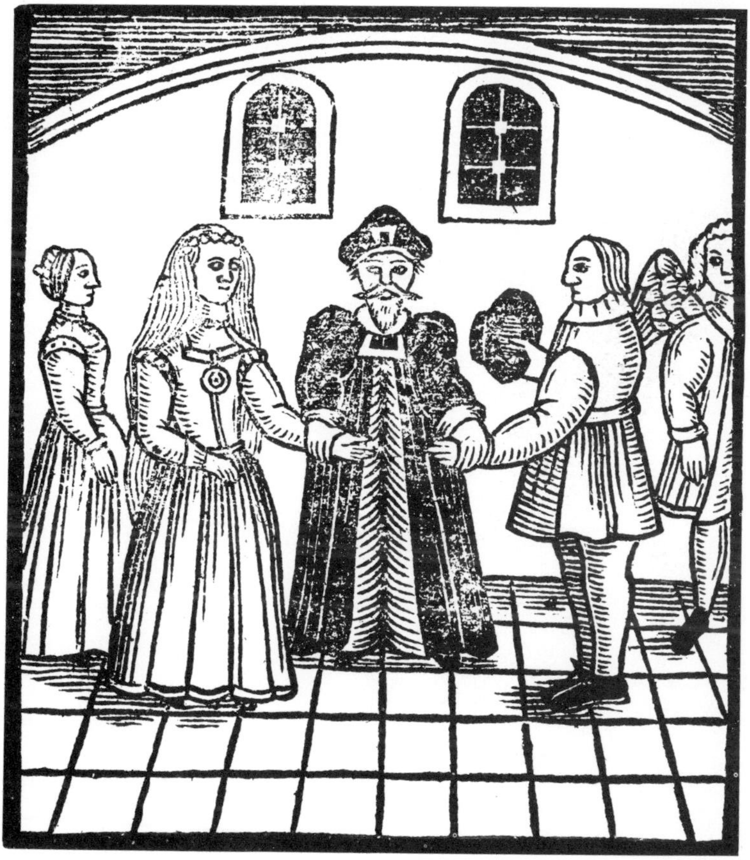

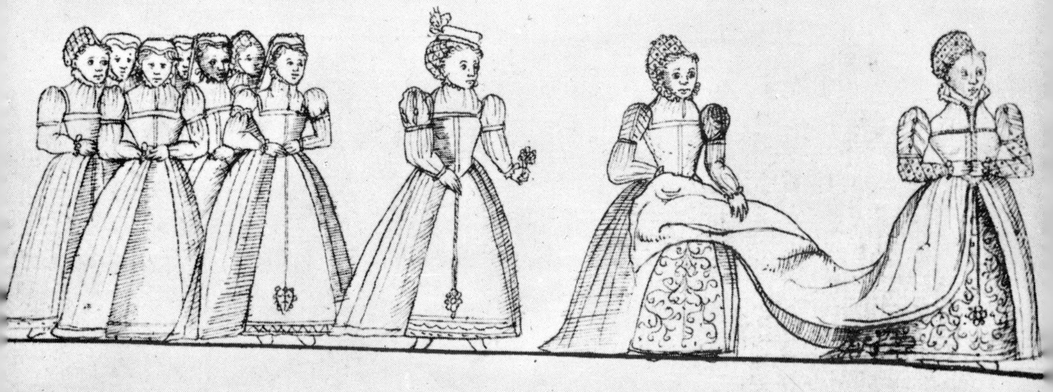

70

Family Pastimes

In Tudor times, there was no cinema or television, no radio or record players, no newspapers or magazines. People had to amuse themselves. The rich were certainly better off than the poor. Wealthy noblemen and ladies who did not have to work, had many ways of passing the time pleasantly. They enjoyed rich banquets with plenty of food and wine. Afterwards, they took part in dancing, singing and pageants. Queen Elizabeth herself enjoyed hunting deer. Hunting was a favourite pastime of rich people, as was falconing and hawking.

But poorer people spent most of Monday to Saturday at work and had little time for fun. They enjoyed themselves most on Sunday afternoons at village festivals such as weddings, fairs and feast days. Everyone looked forward to May Day and for Londoners there was the busy Lord Mayor's Show.

In one way, the people of Tudor times were more clever than we are. Many of them could sing and play musical instruments, and they loved to play for themselves and for one another. But not all entertainment was homemade. During the reign of Elizabeth, for example, plays became very popular. Londoners crowded to the Globe Theatre for the first productions of William Shakespeare's (1564–1616) plays. Rich and poor alike enjoyed the theatre perhaps more than we do today.

72

MASQUES. The *masque* was a magnificent and costly entertainment, enjoyed only by the court and a few noble households. It was a play which included music, singing and formal dancing. It took place against beautiful scenery built and painted by famous architects and artists. The parts in the masque were played by the lords and ladies themselves. In the opposite picture, the masquers are proceeding up the stairs to entertain their friends in the banqueting hall. After the defeat of the Spanish Armada in 1588, masques performed on water became very popular. The opposite picture below shows a masque given in honour of Queen Elizabeth in 1591. You can see her on her throne on the left.

FEASTING. This lively party is taking place in the great hall of a nobleman's house. The meal has come to an end and the couple in front are dancing a stately dance, a *pavane* or *galliard* to the tune of the lute. A group of musicians in the minstrels' gallery at the back of the hall are playing music for all the guests.

COUNTRY DANCES. People of Tudor times enjoyed different kinds of dancing. Rich people in their great houses liked stately and complicated dances. But villagers enjoyed simple *round dances* like the one above. Country dancing took place on the village green, and it was very lively and noisy. After the dancing, the villagers would have an outdoor feast.

MORRIS DANCING. The man above is dancing a *morris dance*, accompanied by a musician with a pipe and drum. The performers of the morris dance were called *mummers*. They wore bells on their legs which jingled as they danced and they waved coloured scarves in the air. The mummers took the part of different characters —the favourite ones were Robin Hood, the Queen of the May, the Fool, a hobby-horse and a dragon. Below, you can see morris dancers near the Thames at Richmond. One dancer is dressed as a hobby-horse.

STREET MUSICIANS. The musicians above are playing the viols for the people eating their meal in the tavern. You can see that viols were played with a bow like the violin. Notice that the two players hold their instruments differently. There were treble, tenor and bass viols. The larger instrument in this picture is a tenor viol; it has a deeper sound than the smaller treble viol. A *consort* of viols consisted of two of each kind. Villagers and townsfolk could listen to these bands of street musicians in the market place, on the village green or in taverns.

MUSIC MAKING OUTSIDE. In the opposite picture, a group of friends are enjoying their music making in the countryside. The man on the right is playing the lute. The lute was one of the most popular instruments in Tudor times. It could be played either on its own or as an accompaniment to a singer. It was pear shaped and had six strings which the player plucked with the fingers. The man in the tree is playing a very odd shaped instrument indeed. What do you think it is?

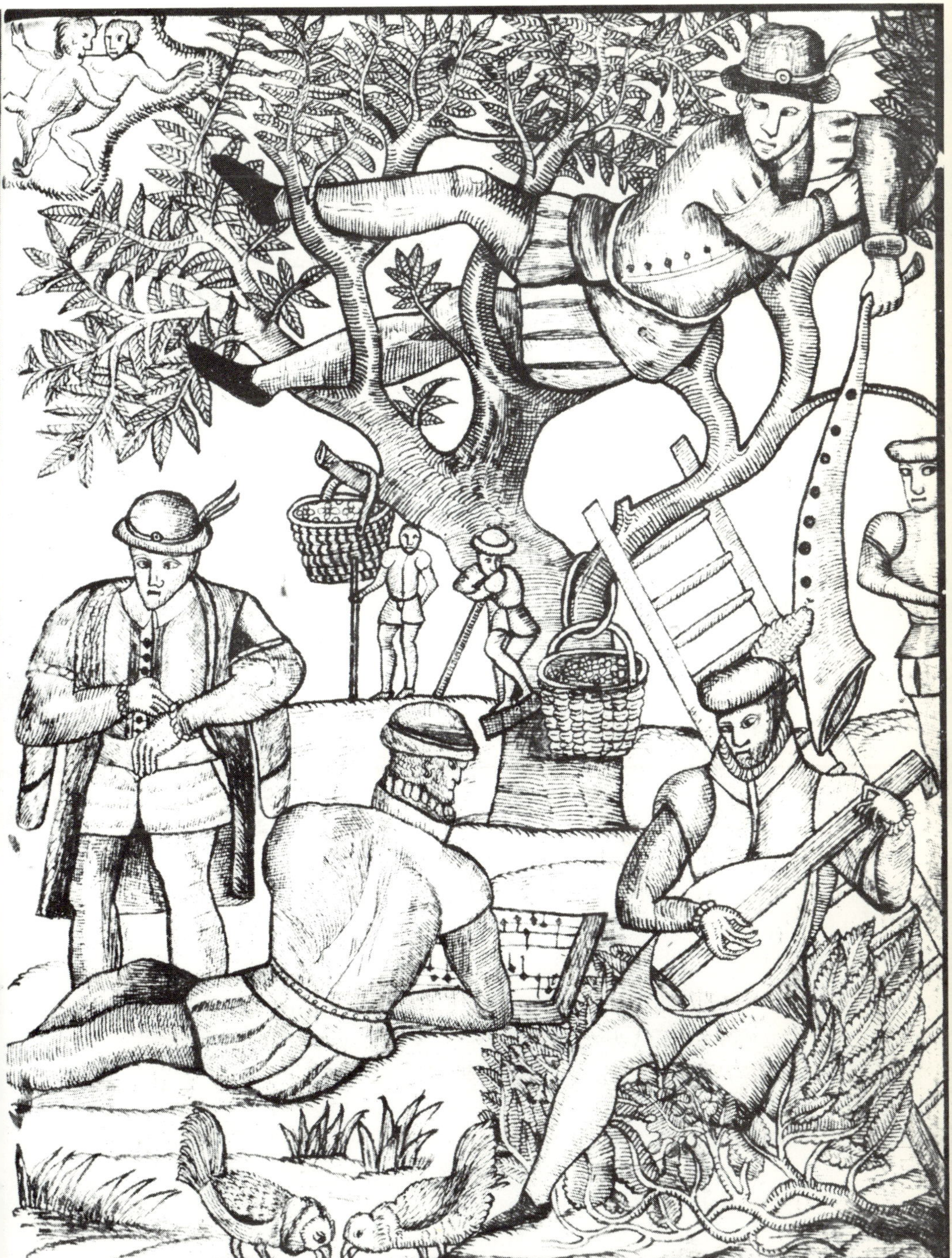

SINGING. Tudor families liked to sing in their homes to entertain themselves, and they also liked to sing in church. Notice the large song book in this church—several people could play or sing from it at once. The men on the left are playing curved instruments called *crumhorns*. The other musician is playing a *clarion* which was a sort of trumpet. The small boys standing in front of the clarion player are choir boys.

WEDDINGS. People in Tudor times loved feast days and a wedding was always a good occasion for a celebration. On the right we can see a wedding feast at Bermondsey. Today it is a part of London, but in those days it was a small village outside the City. A long table has been set out for the feast, and in the kitchen, the servants are preparing the meal. Under the tree a group of musicians are playing a merry jig for the dancers.

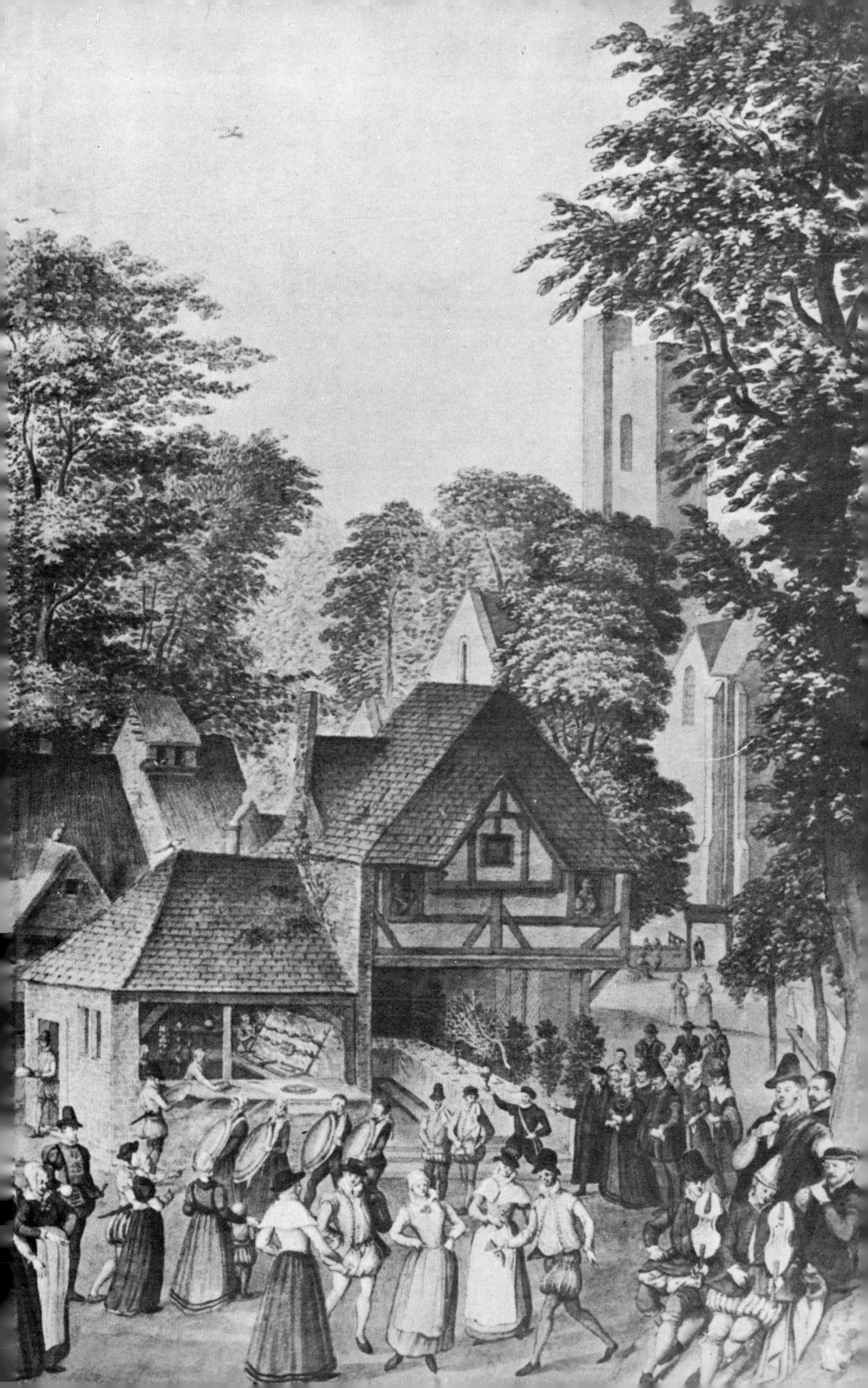

IACOBVS DEI GRATIA REX
SCOTORVM AETATIS SVAE 8
1574

HAWKING. Hawking or falconing was a favourite pastime of wealthy Tudor gentlemen. In the picture above you can see a huntsman holding a falcon. He is wearing one of the well-padded leather gauntlets, or gloves, on which the falcons perched. Falcons were carefully trained to catch many kinds of birds. This falcon is wearing a decorated hood so that it cannot see and will not be tempted to chase a bird before the huntsman is ready. The picture on the left shows James I as a child holding his own falcon.

TENNIS. Wealthy people liked to play tennis, and some great houses had indoor courts. The tennis of those times was not the same as modern lawn tennis. Tudor gentlemen played with a very hard ball inside a walled court. They were allowed to hit the ball against the ceiling and walls, rather like a game of squash. Today you can still go and see a game of Tudor tennis at Henry VIII's palace at Hampton Court.

FOOTBALL. People of Tudor times enjoyed ball games just as much as we do today. Football was often a rough and violent game, with any number of players in a team. Sometimes whole villages played against each other. There would be no marked boundaries for the game. Instead the villagers ran all over the fields as they played. In this picture the players are blowing up the football like a balloon.

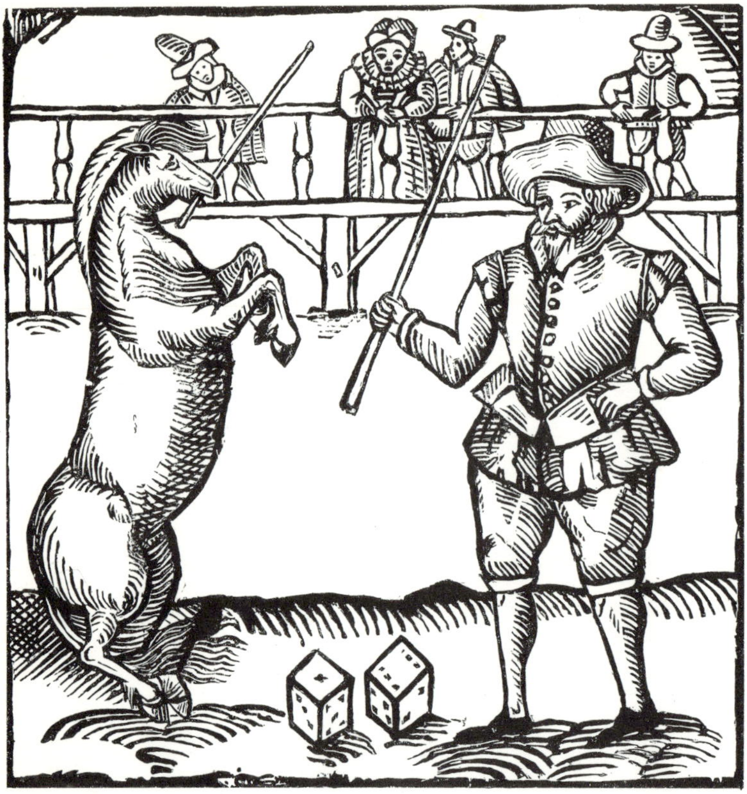

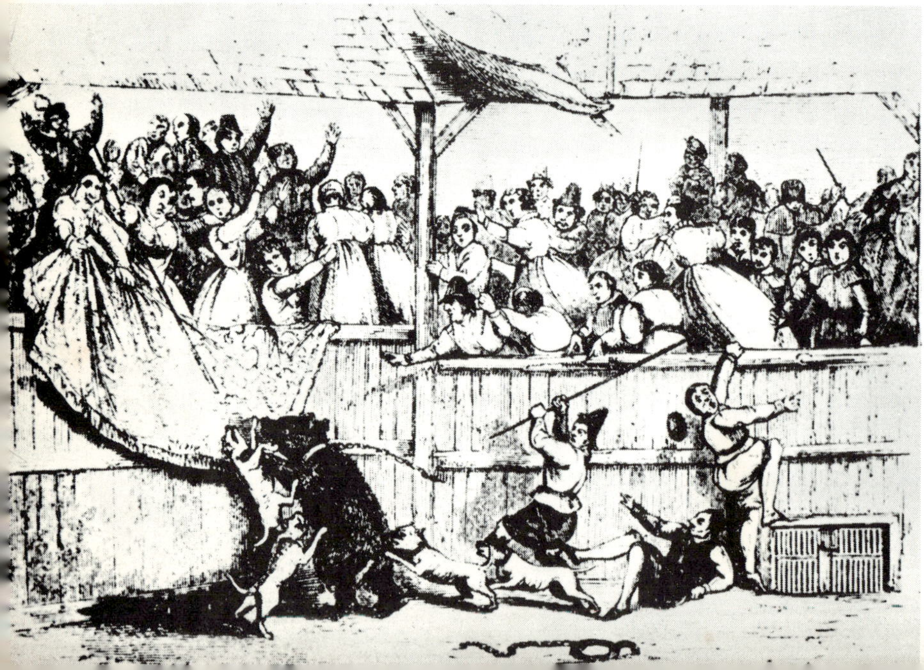

PERFORMING HORSES. Animals were an important part of entertainment in Tudor times. Londoners liked to visit the zoo at the Tower of London where they could see three lionesses, one tiger, a lynx, a wolf, a porcupine and an eagle. On the left is a performing horse who entertained Londoners during Elizabeth's reign. One of his tricks was to tell the audience the uppermost number on a pair of dice. He did this by tapping the number on the ground with his hoof.

BEAR-BAITING. Tudor people were not always kind to animals. Cruel sports like *bear-baiting* and *cock-fighting* were very popular. The lower picture on the opposite page shows a bear-baiting scene. The poor bear has been chained to a post, and the dogs attacking him will soon kill him. Bear-baiting took place in a round building called a bear garden. Below is a famous bear garden which was on the south bank of the River Thames in London, near the Globe theatre.

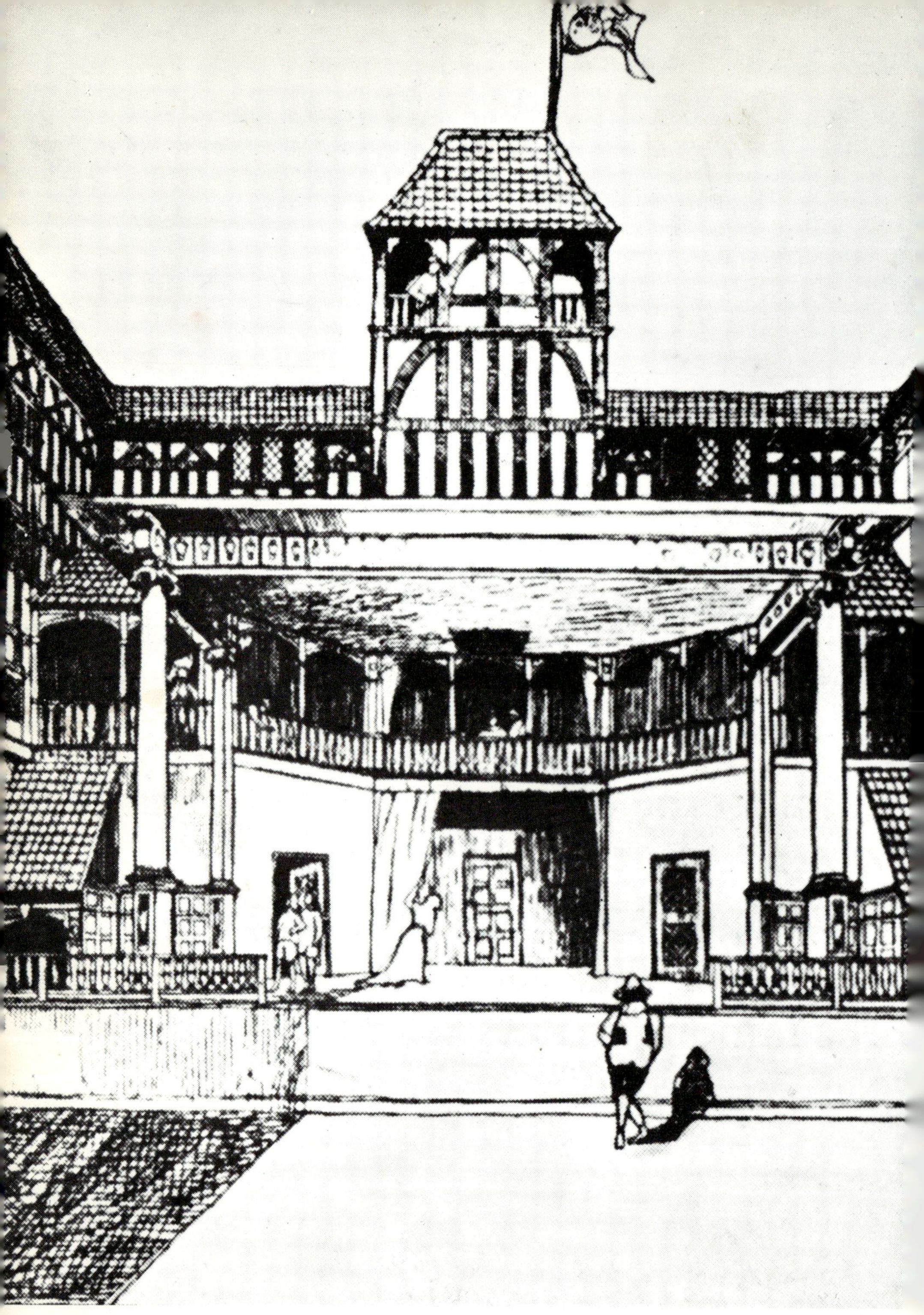

THEATRES. One of the first theatres to be built in London was the Globe. It was just south of the Thames, as you can see from the picture above. Many Elizabethan theatres were round in shape, and the actors were entirely surrounded by the audience. The stage jutted out into the pit where the poorer members of the audience stood. Richer people sat in the galleries. You can see the pit and galleries in the opposite picture. The theatre was open to the sky and performances were given in daylight. It was difficult to perform plays at night because the only light came from torches and candles. Women were not allowed on the stage in the sixteenth century, so boys played all girls' and women's parts.

STROLLING PLAYERS. Not all plays in Tudor times took place in theatres. Performances were often acted in the courtyard of an inn and the stage was put up at one end of the courtyard. The actors had to collect as much money as they could from the crowd below, while the innkeeper took the money from the audience in the gallery. There were also groups of actors, called strolling players, like the ones in this picture, who travelled around the countryside. They put on plays in market places for villagers and townsfolk. Sometimes a nobleman would hire them to perform a play in his great house.

CHURCHGOING. Many of the dancing and merry-making scenes you have seen in this chapter took place on religious holidays. The church was a very important part of life for the Tudor family. Everyone had to go to church on Sunday. If people did not attend, the church-warden would make them pay a fine. Most people were baptized when they were babies, but here a grown-up man is being baptized by the Archbishop of Canterbury. The people on the left are listening to a sermon.

Here lyeth ye bodye of John Selwyn gent kepper of her maties parke of Otelande under ye right honorable Charles Howlwarde Lord Admyrall of England his good Lord & Mr. Who had issue by Susan his wyfe 6 sonnes & vj daughters. all lyving at his death and departed out of this world the xxijth daye of Marche anno Domini. 1587.

TUDOR BRASSES. When Tudor people died, they were buried in the churchyard. Noble families were sometimes buried in a vault inside the church, and their tombs often had pictures of the family made in brass. Here you can see a brass of John Selwyn and his wife Susan with all their children standing between them. During his life, John Selwyn was a keen huntsman and this is shown by the picture on his tomb. If you go into an old country church, look for brasses on the walls or on the floor. They will show you what a Tudor family looked like and how they lived.

Table of Dates

1485   Battle of Bosworth. Henry Tudor defeats Richard III and becomes Henry VII, the first Tudor king
1492   Christopher Columbus sails west and discovers America
1509   Henry VIII becomes King
1534   Henry VIII closes down the monasteries in England
1547   Edward VI is crowned King at the age of nine
1549   First English Prayer Book
1553   Mary Tudor becomes Queen
1558   Elizabeth I, daughter of Henry VIII and Anne Boleyn, becomes Queen
1577   Sir Francis Drake begins his voyage round the world in his ship the *Golden Hind*
1587   Mary Queen of Scots is executed for treason
1588   Defeat of the Spanish Armada by the English navy and Sir Francis Drake
1594   William Shakespeare's first play, *The Comedy of Errors*, is performed at Gray's Inn, London
1598   The Globe Theatre is built in London
1603   Death of Queen Elizabeth after forty-five years of reign. End of the Tudor dynasty.

New Words

Bear-baiting	A cruel sport in which a bear was attacked by dogs
Clarion	An instrument like a trumpet
Cock fighting	Sport in which two cocks were made to fight each other
Consort of viols	A group of instruments like violins, played together
Courtier	A nobleman who attended the king or queen at court
Crumhorn	A kind of flute which was curved up at the end
Doublet	A short tight-fitting jacket worn by men
Dowry	A gift of money or goods which a bride's parents gave to her new husband
Farthingale	A wire hoop worn under the woman's petticoat to make her skirt stand out
Footpad	Thief who roamed the streets at night, attacking passersby
Galliard	A lively dance for two people
Knot garden	A garden of herbs and shrubs planted in a pattern like a knot
Lute	An instrument with strings which were strummed like a guitar
Masque	An entertainment with acting, dancing and beautiful scenery, performed by lords and ladies

Morris dance	A popular country dance
Muffler	A scarf which country women wore over their mouths to keep out the dust
Mummers	People who took part in a morris dance
Pavanne	A slow stately dance performed by lords and ladies
Petty school	A school where very young children learned to read and write
Progress	A journey of inspection made by the king or queen to different parts of the kingdom
Puritans	People who wished to purify the Church of England
Round dance	A merry country dance in which people joined hands in a circle
Tudor	The period from 1485 to 1603 when the Tudor kings and queens ruled England
Virginals	An instrument like a piano with strings which were plucked with quills
Viol	An instrument with a bow played like a violin

More Books

Dodd, A. H. *Life in Elizabethan England* (Batsford, 1961). A detailed picture of life in Tudor times. For older readers.

Harrison, M. & Royston, O. M. *How They Lived* (Blackwell, 1965). Descriptions of life in Tudor England written by people of the time. For older readers.

Makower, F. *People of the Past (the Sixteenth Century)* (O.U.P., 1966). Good stories about the lives of different people in Tudor England.

Quennell, M. & C. H. B. *A History of Everyday Things in England* (Batsford, 1969). Good descriptions of houses, food, clothes and articles of everyday life.

Rosaro, M. *The Life and Times of Elizabeth I* (Hamlyn, 1967). A well illustrated history of Elizabeth's reign. For older readers.

Sutcliff, R. *Brother Dusty Feet* (O.U.P., 1952). An exciting story about a boy who becomes a travelling player (actor).

Taylor, D. *The Elizabethan Age* (Dobson, 1968). A well illustrated book about daily life in Tudor England.

Trease, G. *A Masque for the Queen* (Hamish Hamilton, 1970). A vivid story about Queen Elizabeth's stay with a noble family.

Williams-Ellis, A. & Stobbs, W. *Tudor England* (Blackie, 1968). A good account of the historical events of the Tudor period, with many illustrations.

Index

Actors, 87, 88
Apprentices, 7, 47, 53
Archery, 44, 57

Bear-baiting, 85
Bellman, 38
Blacksmiths, 42
Bible, 45
Brasses, 90
Breeches, 28, 48

Clarion, 78
Court, 9, 27, 29, 30, 55, 73
Crumhorn, 78
Church, 27, 68, 78, 89, 90

Dancing, 64, 73, 74, 75, 78,
Doublet, 48
Dowry, 68
Dyeing, 41

Eastcheap, 20
Elizabeth I, 9, 11, 17, 19, 29, 61, 71, 73

Falconing, 71, 81
Farmers, 21, 23, 27, 38, 40, 41, 43, 61, 64
Farthingale, 8
Feasting, 13, 15, 71, 73

Fencing, 57
Firemen, 37
Fishing, 52
Football, 32, 83

Games, 49, 51
Gardens, 17
Gentleman, 47, 55
Gentlewoman, 17, 62
Great hall, 12
Great houses, 11
Globe Theatre, 71, 85, 87

Hawking, 71, 81
Haymaking, 23
Highwayman, 33

Inns, 34, 88

Jousting, 30, 48

Kitchens, 21, 58

Loom, 24, 64
Lord Mayor of London, 31, 71
Lute, 63, 76

Markets, 7, 20 23
Masques, 73

95

May Day, 64, 71
Merchants, 27, 31, 32, 47
Morris dancing, 75
Muffler, 19, 23
Mummer, 75
Music, 63, 73, 76

Needlework, 14

Page boys, 55

Raleigh, Sir Walter 35
Royal Exchange, 32

Servants, 7, 11, 15, 20, 21, 27, 66
Schools, 48, 49, 61
Shakespeare, William, 71

Shepherds, 59
Shops, 7, 34
Singing, 63, 71, 78
Spanish Armada, 73
Spinning, 14, 24, 27, 64
Soldiers, 44
Street sellers, 36
Strolling players, 88

Tailor, 34, 53
Tennis, 82
Tobacco, 34

Veterinary surgeon, 43
Viols, 63, 76

Weaving, 24, 64
Weddings, 68, 78
Wool, 24, 27, 41, 64

PICTURE CREDITS

The Publishers wish to thank the following for their kind permission to reproduce copyright illustrations on the pages mentioned: The Marquess of Salisbury, K.G., *jacket*,; the Mansell Collection, 8, 12, 20, 54, 62, 64; the Radio-Times Hulton Picture Library, 14, 15, 21, 22 (top), 24, 30 (top), 33, 37, 40, 44, 46, 48 (bottom), 49, 50, 55, 58, 59, 60, 63 (bottom), 66 (top), 73, 78, 83, 86, 87, 89, 90; John Freeman Ltd., 16 (top), 28, 29 (top), 39, 48 (top), 51, 52, 56 (bottom), 69, 74; British Publishing Corporation, 70; Trustees of the Fitzwilliam Museum, 75 (bottom); the Fogler Library, 77; Trustees of the British Museum, *frontispiece*, 18, 22 (bottom), 25, 31, 41, 53, 67, 88; Trustees of the National Portrait Gallery, 6, 9, 26, 29 (bottom), 72 (top), 80; Trustees of the Tate Museum, 10; Trustees of the Victoria and Albert Museum, 13; Trustees of the London Museum, 68, 79.